Parenting

Raising Faithful Older Adolescents

Augsburg Fortress, Minneapolis

Contents

INTERSECTIONS
Small Group Series

Parenting
Raising Faithful Older Adolescents

Developed in cooperation with the Division for Congregational Ministries, ELCA

George S. Johnson, series introduction
John Roberto, Center for Ministry Development editor
Contributors: Audrey Taylor and Joe Taylor
Editors: Laurie J. Hanson and Elizabeth Drotning
The Wells Group, series design
Cover photo: © 2001 Visual Images

Page 14, 20, 26, 32, 39, 45 photos © 2001 PhotoDisc

Materials identified as *LBW* are from *Lutheran Book of Worship*, copyright 1978.

Scripture quotations are from New Revised Standard Version Bible, copyright 1989 Division of Christian Education of the National Council of the Churches of Christ in the United States of America. Used by permission.

1 2 3 4 5 6 7 8 9 0 1 2 3 4 5 6 7 8 9

Introduction

A quick look at the family section of your local bookstore will reveal dozens of books about parenting. What you probably will not find among these titles is a book about parenting and faith growth. *Parenting: Raising Faithful Older Adolescents* is specifically designed for parents of high school youth. It provides an understanding of the unique characteristics of young people and ideas and strategies for nurturing faith in their lives by sharing Christian values, celebrating rituals, praying together, serving those in need, and developing a strong family life. *Parenting: Raising Faithful Older Adolescents* also suggests ways that you can continue growing as you walk with your teenager in faith.

This book provides you with an understanding of the unique characteristics of older adolescents and the challenges and opportunities for parenting at this stage of life. Older adolescents are caught up in the challenges presented by new ways of thinking, an expanded circle of contacts and friends, greater autonomy, and the need to redefine relationships. But they still need your concern and care. You can continue to have an influence on their faith and values, and grow with them in the process.

This book and your small group can help you develop your parenting skills and find support and encouragement for growing in faith and raising faithful older adolescents.

Developmental assets

Search Institute, a research and educational organization in Minneapolis, has compiled a list of 40 developmental assets for elementary-aged children. (See page 52.) These assets are components identified in the lives of healthy, happy, well-adjusted children. They are named in this course as an awareness-raising guide as we work to raise healthy, faithful children.

Baptismal promises

This baptismal symbol appears in each chapter next to activities that remind us of the promises we make when our children are baptized.

SMALL GROUP SERIES

Welcome into the family of those who are part of small groups! Intersections Small Group Series will help you and other members of your group build relationships and discover ways to connect the Christian faith with your everyday life.

This book is prepared for those who want to make a difference in this world, who want to grow in their Christian faith, as well as for those who are beginning to explore the Christian faith. The information in this introduction to the Intersections small group experience can help your group make the most out of your time together.

Biblical encouragement

Do not be conformed to this world, but be transformed by the renewing of your minds, so that you may discern what is the will of God—what is good and acceptable and perfect. Romans 12:2.

Small groups provide an atmosphere where the Holy Spirit can transform lives. As you share your life stories and learn together, God's Spirit can work to enlighten and direct you.

Strength is provided to face the pressures to conform to forces and influences that are opposed to what is "good and acceptable and perfect." To "be transformed" is an ongoing experience of God's grace as we take up the cross and follow Jesus. Changed lives happen as we live in community with one another. Small groups encourage such change and growth.

What is a small group?

A number of definitions and descriptions of the small group ministry experience exist throughout the church. Roberta Hestenes, a Presbyterian pastor and author, defines a small group as an intentional face-to-face gathering of three to twelve people who meet regularly with the common purpose of discovering and growing in the possibilities of the abundant life.

Whatever definition you use, the following characteristics are important.

Small—Seven to ten people is ideal so that everyone can be heard and no one's voice is lost. More than twelve members makes genuine caring difficult.

Intentional—Commitment to the group is a high priority.

Personal—Sharing experiences and insights is more important than mastering content.

Conversational—Leaders that facilitate conversation, rather than teach, are the key to encouraging participation.

Friendly—Having a warm, accepting, nonjudgmental atmosphere is essential.

Christ-centered—The small-group experience is biblically based, related to the real world, and founded on Christ.

Features of Intersections Small Group Series

A small-group model

A number of small-group ministry models exist. Most models include three types of small groups:

- *Discipleship groups*—where people gather to grow in Christian faith and life;

- *Support and recovery groups*—which focus on special interests, concerns, or needs; and

- *Ministry groups*—which have a task-oriented focus.

Intersections Small Group Series offers material for all of these.

For discipleship groups, this series offers a variety of courses with Bible study at the center. What makes a discipleship group different from traditional group Bible studies? In discipleship groups, members bring their life experience to the exploration of the biblical material.

For support and recovery groups, Intersections Small Group Series offers topical material to assist group members in dealing with issues related to their common experience, hurt, or interest. An extra section of facilitator helps in the back of the book will assist leaders of support and recovery groups to anticipate and prepare for special circumstances and needs that may arise as group members explore a topic.

Ministry groups can benefit from an environment that includes prayer, biblical reflection, and relationship building, in addition to their task focus.

Four essentials

Prayer, personal sharing, biblical reflection, and a group ministry task are part of each time you gather. These are all important for Christian community to be experienced. Each of the six chapter themes in each book includes:

- Short prayers to open and close your time together.

- Carefully worded questions to make personal sharing safe, nonthreatening, and voluntary.

- A biblical base from which to understand and discover the power and grace of God. God's Word is the compass that keeps the group on course.

- A group ministry task to encourage both individuals and the group as a whole to find ways to put faith into action.

Flexibility

Each book contains six chapter themes that may be covered in six sessions or easily extended for groups that meet for a longer period of time. Each chapter theme is organized around two to three main topics with supplemental material to make it easily adaptable to your small group's needs. You need not use all the material. Most themes will work well for 1½- to 2-hour sessions, but a variety of scheduling options is possible.

Bible-based

Each of the six chapter themes in the book includes one or more Bible texts printed in its entirety from the New Revised Standard Version of the Bible. This makes it easy for all group members to read and learn from the same text. Participants will be encouraged through questions, with exercises, and by other group members to address biblical texts in the context of their own lives.

User-friendly

The material is prepared in such a way that it is easy to follow, practical, and does not require a professional to lead it. Designating one to be the facilitator to guide the group is important, but there is no requirement for this person to be theologically trained or an expert in the course topic. Many times options are given so that no one will feel forced into any set way of responding.

Group goals and process

1. Creating a group covenant or contract for your time together will be important. During your first meeting, discuss these important characteristics of all small groups and decide how your group will handle them.

Confidentiality—Agreeing that sensitive issues that are shared remain in the group.

Regular attendance—Agreeing to make meetings a top priority.

Nonjudgmental behavior—Agreeing to confess one's own shortcomings, if appropriate, not those of others, and not giving advice unless asked for it.

Prayer and support—Being sensitive to one another, listening, becoming a caring community.

Accountability—Being responsible to each other and open to change.

Items in your covenant should be agreed upon by all members. Add to the group covenant as you go along. Space to record key aspects is included in the back of this book. See page 51.

2. Everyone is responsible for the success of the group, but do arrange to have one facilitator who can guide the group process each time you meet.

The facilitator is not a teacher or healer. Teaching, learning, and healing happen from the group experience. The facilitator is more of a shepherd who leads the flock to where they can feed and drink and feel safe.

Remember, an important goal is to experience genuine love and community in a Christ-centered atmosphere. To help make this happen, the facilitator encourages active listening and honest sharing. This person allows the material to facilitate opportunities for self-awareness and interaction with others.

Leadership is shared in a healthy group, but the facilitator is the one designated to set the pace, keep the group focused, and enable the members to support and care for each other.

People need to sense trust and freedom as the group develops; therefore, avoid "shoulds" or "musts" in your group.

3. Taking on a group ministry task can help members of your group balance personal growth with service to others.

In your first session, identify ways your group can offer help to others within the congregation or in your surrounding community. Take time at each meeting to do or arrange for that ministry task. Many times it is in the doing that we discover what we believe or how God is working in our lives.

4. Starting or continuing a personal action plan offers a way to address personal needs that you become aware of in your small-group experience.

For example, you might want to spend more time in conversation with a friend or spouse. Your action plan might state, "I plan to visit with Terry two times before our next small-group meeting."

If you decide to pursue a personal action plan, consider sharing it with your small group. Your group can be helpful in at least three ways: by giving support; helping to define the plan in realistic, measurable ways; and offering a source to whom you can be accountable.

5. Prayer is part of small-group fellowship. There is great power in group prayer, but not everyone feels free to offer spontaneous prayer. That's okay.

Learning to pray aloud takes time and practice. If you feel uncomfortable, start with simple and short prayers. And remember to pray for other members between sessions.

Use page 51 in the back of this book to note prayer requests made by group members.

6. Consider using a journal to help reflect on your experiences and insights between meeting times.

Writing about feelings, ideas, and questions can be one way to express yourself; plus it helps you remember what so often gets lost with time.

The "Daily Walk" component includes material that can get your journaling started. This, of course, is up to you and need not be done on any regular schedule. Even doing it once a week can be time well spent.

How to use this book

The material provided for each session is organized around some key components. If you are the facilitator for your small group, be sure to read this section carefully.

The facilitator's role is to establish a hospitable atmosphere and set a tone that encourages participants to share, reflect, and listen to each other. Some important practical things can help make this happen.

- Whenever possible meet in homes. Be sure to provide clear directions about how to get there.

- Use name tags for several sessions.

- Place the chairs in a circle and close enough for everyone to hear and feel connected.

- Be sure everyone has access to a book; preparation will pay off.

- Have Bibles available and encourage participants to bring their own.

Welcoming

In this study, parents and guardians of older adolescents can come together to explore how to nurture faith in their families and the lives of their teenagers. This study provides a balance between understanding the faith of older adolescents and developing practical ideas and strategies to nurture faith at home. Encourage the participants to put the ideas they explore into practice at home during the week. Parents and guardians of teenagers need encouragement and support in their efforts to build a family of faith.

Make necessary arrangements so that the physical and emotional environment for this group is as relaxed and comfortable as possible. Encourage people to come as they are, whether in business suits or gardening clothes. Make arrangements for child-care options to be available. Seek volunteer caregivers or shared child-care opportunities so that financial constraints do not keep people from attending.

Create a cozy atmosphere. Comfortable seating and space where everyone can converse with one another and be part of the group is vital. Encourage people to bring photos of their children to share with the group.

Focus

Each of the six chapter themes in this book has a brief focus statement. Read it aloud. It will give everyone a sense of the direction for each session and provide some boundaries so that people will not feel lost or frustrated trying to cover everything. The focus also connects the theme to the course topic.

Community building

This opening activity is crucial to a relaxed, friendly atmosphere. It will prepare the ground for gradual group development. Two "Community Building" options are provided under each theme. With the facilitator giving his or her response to the questions first, others are free to follow.

One purpose for this section is to allow everyone to participate as he or she responds to nonthreatening questions. The activity serves as a check-in time when participants are invited to share how things are going or what is new.

Make this time light and fun; remember, humor is a welcome gift. Use fifteen to twenty minutes for this activity in your first few sessions and keep the entire group together.

During your first meeting, encourage group members to write down names and phone numbers (when appropriate) of the other members, so people can keep in touch. Use page 50 for this purpose.

Discovery

This component focuses on exploring the theme for your time together, using material that is read and questions and exercises that encourage sharing of personal insights and experiences.

Reading material includes a Bible text with supplemental passages and commentary written by the topic writer. Have volunteers read the Bible texts aloud. The main passage to be used is printed so that everyone operates from a common translation and sees the text.

"A Further Look" is included in some places to give you additional study material if time permits. Use it to explore related passages and questions. Be sure to have extra Bibles handy.

Questions and exercises related to the theme will invite personal sharing and storytelling. Keep in mind that as you listen to each other's stories, you are inspired to live more fully in the grace and will of God. Such exchanges make Christianity relevant and transformation more likely to happen. Caring relationships are key to clarifying one's beliefs. Sharing personal experiences and insights is what makes the small group spiritually satisfying.

Most people are open to sharing their life stories, especially if they're given permission to do so and they know someone will actively listen. Starting with the facilitator's response usually works best. On some occasions you may want to break the group into units of three or four persons to explore certain questions. When you reconvene, relate your experience to the whole group. The phrase "explore and relate," which appears occasionally in the margin, refers to this recommendation. If your group includes couples, encourage them to separate for this smaller group activity. Appoint someone to start the discussion.

Wrap-up

Plan your schedule so that there will be enough time for wrapping up. This time can include work on your group ministry task, review of key discoveries during your time together, identifying personal and prayer concerns, closing prayers, and the Lord's Prayer.

The facilitator can help the group identify and plan its ministry task. Introduce the idea and decide on your group ministry task in the first session. Tasks need not be grandiose. Activities might include:

- Ministry in your community, such as adopting a food shelf, clothes closet, or homeless shelter; sponsoring equipment, food, or clothing drives; or sending members to staff the shelter.

- Ministry to members of the congregation, such as writing notes to those who are ill or bereaved.

- Congregational tasks where volunteers are always needed, such as serving refreshments during the fellowship time after worship, stuffing envelopes for a church mailing, or taking responsibility for altar preparations for one month.

Depending upon the task, you can use part of each meeting time to carry out or plan the task.

In the "Wrap-up," allow time for people to share insights and encouragement and to voice special prayer requests. Just to mention someone who needs prayer is a form of prayer. The "Wrap-up" time may include a brief worship experience with candles, prayers, and singing. You might form a circle and hold hands. Silence can be effective. If you use the Lord's Prayer in your group, select the version that is known in your setting. There is space on page 50 to record the version your group uses. Another closing prayer is also printed on page 50. Before you go, ask members to pray for one another during the week. Remember also any special concerns or prayer requests.

Daily walk

Seven Bible readings and a verse, thought, and prayer for the journey related to the material just discussed are provided for those who want to keep the theme before them between sessions. These brief readings may be used for devotional time. Some group members may want to memorize selected passages. The Bible readings also can be used for supplemental study by the group if needed. Prayer for other group members also can be part of this time of personal reflection.

A word of encouragement

No material is ever complete or perfect for every situation or group. Creativity and imagination will be important gifts for the facilitator to bring to each theme. Keep in mind that it is in community that we are challenged to grow in Jesus Christ. Together we become what we could not become alone. It is God's plan that it be so.

For additional resources and ideas see *Starting Small Groups—and Keeping Them Going* (Minneapolis: Augsburg Fortress, 1995).

1 Nurturing the Faith of Older Adolescents

Focus

As parents, we can continue to have an influence on the faith and values of our teenagers and grow with them in the process.

Community building

Option

Think back to the time when you were 15 or 16 years old. How important was God or religion to you? How did you feel about church? Would you like to be 15 or 16 again?

Introduce yourselves to one another. Share your teenagers' names and ages. Then share responses to these unfinished sentences with each other.

- One of the best things about being a parent of a teenager is…

- One of the most challenging things about being a parent of a teenager is…

- One thing I've learned from my teenager is…

- One thing I still need to learn as a parent of a teenager is…

Read the prayer together.

Opening prayer

Loving God, we give you thanks for our teenagers—for their hopes and dreams, their energy and spirit. Open our eyes to the marvelous potential in our teenagers and help us to see you at work in their lives each day.
Amen

A time of changes and challenges

Adolescence ushers in a new era in family life brought on by new life tasks and the changing role of parents in relationship to their teenagers. The changes of adolescence—puberty, new ways of thinking, a wider sphere of social activity and relationships, greater autonomy—present the family as a whole with a new set of challenges. Take a moment to think about several of the incredible changes happening in the lives of teenagers.

- Take a moment to think about the growth that your teenager is experiencing. Identify several changes that are happening in his or her life today.

- As a group, describe important characteristics of the teenage years.

Teenagers are growing intellectually, developing the ability to reflect on what they think and why they think that way. This growth helps teenagers develop their own identities, value systems, and faith, as well as thinking about and planning for their future. While this is happening, teenagers may have periods of self-centeredness or a desire to be alone. They also use their new abilities to challenge rules, push limits, and question and challenge their parents' values and ideas. This makes relationships and communication more difficult for both parents and older adolescents.

Teenagers are beginning to establish a personal identity—their own values and sense of self. They develop greater degrees of independence in making personal decisions and assuming responsibility for their lives, and experiment with different behaviors, attitudes, and ideas. They are also concerned with and focused on developing their sexual identity. As they establish their own identity, older adolescents are still shaped and influenced by the values and faith of their families. The challenge for parents is to allow for the increasing independence of adolescents while maintaining enough structure to foster continued healthy growth.

Teenagers are developing a personal moral code to guide their behavior. They are examining and reevaluating the moral values received from family, church, and significant others, as they seek to develop personal responsibility. During this time, they are still influenced by values and faith shared during childhood and lived by parents and adult role models in the present.

Teenagers are expanding their social world beyond family to a variety of friendship groups. They are developing the capability for more mutual, trusting, deep, and enduring personal relationships. Friendships help teens experience belonging, support, and acceptance. Friends validate teens' decisions and support their new independent selves. As the social world of older adolescents expands, relationships with parents are often redefined.

Teenagers are exploring and questioning the faith handed down by family and church. They are trying to figure out how God fits into their lives and wondering about life and death, the meaning and purpose in life, and so forth. Many teenagers begin to take responsibility for their own faith life, commitments, and beliefs.

Because it is often a struggle, parents are often tempted to focus on a destination—the end of the older adolescent stage. Yet there is much to be said for the journey as well. From the seeds of both our failures and successes, God can harvest much. This is a time when we as parents are challenged to re-think our ideas, listen with every ounce of our being, look inward as well as outward, laugh, reclaim or revise our own values, love unconditionally, forgive, go one more mile when we don't think we have it in us, persevere, and especially to grow. However, we may also find intense joy in this journey.

■ Which insights about teenagers fit with your experience as a parent?

■ What new insights about teenagers did you discover?

■ How does understanding the characteristics of older adolescents help you become a more effective parent?

Luke 6:47-49

Read the scripture passage aloud.

[47]**"I will show you what someone is like who comes to me, hears my words, and acts on them.** [48]**That one is like a man building a house, who dug deeply and laid the foundation on rock; when a flood arose, the river burst against that house but could not shake it, because it had been well built.** [49]**But the one who hears and does not act is like a man who built a house on the ground without a foundation. When the river burst against it, immediately it fell, and great was the ruin of that house."**

Building blocks for growth

Forty developmental assets identified by the Search Institute provide the building blocks that help adolescents grow up to be healthy, well- adjusted, and strong. Just as immunizations keep young people healthy and protect them from disease, these 40 assets help adolescents make healthy choices and inoculate them against a wide range of risk-taking behaviors. The more assets young people have, the more likely they are to be healthy and engage in positive behaviors.

The asset-building approach provides concrete, ways to think about parenting and family life. The "bottom line" in parenting lies in raising caring, competent, and responsible young people.

Group goals and ministry task

Read about group goals and group ministry tasks on pages 6-7. In groups of three, discuss the following questions. Then share your answers in the large group.

- ■ What do you hope to accomplish in this small group course?

- ■ Brainstorm group ministry task ideas that include your older adolescents.

Experiencing ways to reach out in Christ's love is a powerful way to learn. Consider projects aimed at the needs of teenagers, such as mentoring programs, career guidance, and so forth. Record your goals and group ministry task in the appendix on page 51.

Discovery

What every teenager needs from a parent

Read and discuss.

■ What do you consider the essentials that every teenager needs from his or her parents?

Throughout their book, *10 Best Gifts for Your Teen* (Notre Dame, Ind.: Ave Maria Press, 1999), Patt and Steve Saso identify what young people need from parents.

Respect. Respect is the key to a successful parent-teen relationship. Respecting teenagers means to take them seriously, separate what they do from who they are, avoid comparisons, and honor their plans.

Room. Giving teenagers room means allowing them the privacy they need to become their own persons. For example, this could involve allowing older adolescents to maintain their bedrooms in ways that reflect their personalities.

Receptivity. To be receptive to what your teen is saying, become a more attentive and active listener. Stop what you are doing, face your son or daughter, make eye contact, and listen with your full attention.

Revelation of self. Revelation of self means sharing your past and your present, as well as your dreams for the future. When you share about your very human struggles and reflect on your life experiences, you are inviting your son or daughter to do the same. To do this, show interest in your teenager's activities, spend time with them, be vulnerable, and be honest with them.

Responsibility. Teaching your teen to be responsible is a lifelong process. Nurture responsible behavior in teenagers by giving them choices and holding them accountable for the consequences, helping them set goals, giving them responsibilities at home, holding regular family meetings, and modeling responsible behavior.

Resolve. Parenting with resolve means sharing and living out your values, setting clear limits and rules to keep your teen safe, using natural and logical consequences, being consistent and following through when those limits or rules are broken, using mistakes as an opportunity to learn, and building a family support system with other families in your congregation and community.

Recognition. Recognition means honoring teenagers for their successes, hard work, and strengths. Give recognition by affirming positive behavior and personal qualities, expressing love and saying "I love you," trusting in your teenager, attending his or her events, and accepting your teenager for the person he or she is.

Reconciliation. Everyone makes mistakes. By admitting your mistakes and seeking forgiveness, you are doing three things: a) healing a wounded relationship, b) modeling the ability to admit mistakes and seek forgiveness, and c) offering your teenager the opportunity to extend forgiveness. Reconciliation requires respect, sensitivity to feelings, vulnerability, honesty, responsibility, self-discipline, and courage. It is essential to building a trusting, loving relationship with your teenager. As you model for your teen a willingness to ask forgiveness and seek reconciliation, they will be more open to admitting their mistakes. The healing will be mutual.

Release. Release is the gift of "letting go." It means giving teenagers more and more freedom as they get older, encouraging them to be their own person. It is also about helping them grow up, so that by the time you launch your teen into the world of college or career, they will be prepared.

Role-modeling. Our goal as parents is to model the very behaviors we want to see in our teens as they grow into adults.

Reflect on the questions individually and then discuss responses with the group.

■ How many of these ideas were already on your list?

■ What new ideas did you discover? What would you add to your list of essentials?

■ Which of these ideas will you start using right now? How will you start?

To learn more about parenting older adolescents and to find a variety of family activities and ideas, see the resource list on page 54.

A further look

Read the passage and then take time individually to write your own responses. Share insights with the group.

A parent's baptismal promise

At baptism, parents are asked to state what they want for their children. Parents promise to bring up their child in the Christian faith and to teach their child to keep God's commandments as Christ taught us by loving God and neighbor. What do you want for your teenager?

Take a few minutes now or during the week to consider what you want for your teenager. State your intentions clearly. You might even put them in writing.

■ Think ahead to the day your son or daughter is on his or her own. How would you define success as a parent?

■ What role will faith play in their lives?

Evaluate how well-equipped you are to make this happen. Remember Jesus' question to his would-be disciples: "For which of you, intending to build a tower, does not first sit down and estimate the cost, to see whether he has enough to complete it?" (Luke 14:28).

Wrap-up

See page 9 in the intro-
duction for a description
of "Wrap-up."

Before you go, take time for the following:

- Group ministry task

- Review

- Personal concerns and prayer concerns

See page 51 for sug-
gested closing prayers.
Page 51 can also be
used for listing ongoing
prayer requests.

- Closing prayers

Daily walk

Bible readings

Day 1
Matthew 22:34-40

Day 2
John 15:12-17

Day 3
Matthew 5:21-26 and
7:1-5

Day 4
1 Corinthians 13:1-8

Day 5
Colossians 3:12-17

Day 6
Romans 12:9-18

Day 7
1 John 4:7-21

Verse for the journey

Let each of you look not to your own interests, but to the
interests of others. Let the same mind be in you that was in
Christ Jesus. Philippians 2:4-5

Thought for the journey

Because it is often a struggle, parents are often tempted to
focus on a destination—the end of the adolescent stage. Yet
there is much to be said for the journey as well.

Prayer for the journey

Lord, we ask you for the wisdom and insight necessary to be
faith-filled parents of older adolescents. Help us to build
strong relationships with our sons and daughters, nourishing
them with love, care, and a supportive home life. May they
grow to become all you created them to be.
Amen

2 Sharing Faith and Values

Focus

Families share faith and values through words and actions, loving relationships, and a caring environment.

Community building

Reflect on the timeline activity, then have each person tell about one or two key moments from their faith journey.

On the following timeline, identify important dates, events, and people that have strongly affected your faith journey. Be sure to include your teenage and young adult years. Use the following symbols on the timeline:

G = times when God was important to you
? = times of questioning or doubting your faith
+ = times when you grew spiritually
- = times when faith was not important to you
! = times when God's love was revealed to you

Option

With a word, phrase, symbol, or image, describe what your faith meant to you as a teenager and what it means to you today. Why is the Christian faith important to you? Why it is important for you to nurture this faith in your teenagers?

|------------|------------|-------------|-------------|------------|
0   today

Opening prayer

Listen, my people, mark each word. I begin with a story, I speak of mysteries welling up from ancient depths. We must not hide this story from our children but tell the mighty works and all the wonders of God.

Psalm 78:1-4 (adapted)

Deuteronomy 6:4-9

Read the scripture
passage aloud, then
discuss.

4 Hear, O Israel: The Lord is our God, the Lord alone. 5 You shall love the Lord your God with all your heart, and with all your soul, and with all your might. 6 Keep these words that I am commanding you today in your heart. 7 Recite them to your children and talk about them when you are at home and when you are away, when you lie down and when you rise. 8 Bind them as a sign on your hand, fix them as an emblem on your forehead, 9 and write them on the doorposts of your house and on your gates.

▪ What are your hopes for the faith life of your teen?

Read and discuss.

A faith for teenagers

There are many ways for older adolescents to live and grow in faith. They can . . .

  a. trust in God's unconditional love, acceptance, and forgiveness and discover God's presence in each day
  b. find meaning and purpose for their life in a relationship with God
  c. read and apply Scriptures regularly
  d. learn to relate to a loving God in prayer
  e. worship God in a faith community
  f. live values of faith
  g. develop loving relationships built upon values
  h. act as peacemakers and promote reconciliation in their relationships, community, and world
  i. practice stewardship of God's creation, sharing their personal talents and possessions, as well as the resources of the earth
  j. recognize that all people are created by God
  k. participate in efforts to work for social justice and respond to basic human needs
  l. live a life of simplicity free from the pressures of materialism and consumerism

As parents, we need to show that our own faith is important to us. We need to demonstrate to our teenagers that Jesus brings wholeness, liberation, and the certainty of being loved unconditionally and extravagantly by God. We also need to support and encourage teenagers when they realize that following Jesus can involve some sacrifices.

▪ How does the description of a faith for teenagers fit with your hopes for your teen? Would you add anything to the list?

Review the six positive values, assets 26-31, and then discuss the questions.

Consider this

Search Institute has identified six positive values that are essential for healthy growth: caring, equality and social justice, integrity, honesty, responsibility, and healthy lifestyle. Turn to page 53 to read the descriptions of each value in assets 26-31.

■ **Why are these values so important for the healthy, positive growth of older adolescents?**

■ **Which of these values would you like to emphasize more in your family?**

Discovery

Sharing faith with teenagers

Read and discuss.

■ How can we guide teenagers to believe in the Lord, trust God, and live as disciples of Jesus Christ?

There are many ways to share the Christian faith with teenagers:

Set an example with your life. You can't successfully convince your young person to pray, participate in Sunday worship, serve others, and be involved in the church community if you are not setting the example.

Provide a spiritually nurturing home environment. Provide an environment where family members live in God's presence and experience God rather than simply talk about God and practice religious rituals.

Create an atmosphere where your teenager will feel comfortable sharing thoughts and discussing issues that are causing conflict. Be willing to talk about anything and listen carefully to what your teenager is saying. Your family should be a place where your teenager can experience the richness of God's love, acceptance, and forgiveness.

Teach through your daily routine and interactions. The style of your daily routine and interactions say (or leave unsaid) a good deal about your faith and values. Your daily routine shows how you treat others, how you use time, how you eat, how you manage or mismanage money, and how you handle or avoid conflict, as well as how you pray, how you are involved or uninvolved in church, and how you think about and relate to God.

Talk about values. Every time your adolescent asks, "Why?," you have an opportunity to share the values of your faith. For example, when a teen asked her parents, "Why should I declare my waitress tips on income tax forms? No one else does," a meaningful discussion about honesty versus cheating followed. The question, "Why can't we stay overnight in a hotel suite after the prom? It's a whole bunch of couples, not just us two," can lead to a discussion about relationships and sexuality as God-given gifts with responsibilities attached. Special events and milestones, such as anniversaries, graduations, family moves, and job changes, also provide a time to talk about family values and how your family lives them out.

We can encourage our teenagers to ask themselves two questions when making a choice or decision: (1) Will this be a life-giving decision for all involved? (2) Is this a choice or a decision for people or for things?

Discuss crises in the light of faith. Crisis situations are key times to share our faith and display the strength that our faith gives us. Crises involving suffering, illness, loss, or death provide opportunities to connect the life of Jesus, Scriptures, and the Christian tradition to present day realities. Disappointment in another person, failure, anger, shame, and illness are all unplanned circumstances that families need to talk about. Vocational goals, losing a job, good grades, and bad grades represent the ups and downs that are woven into the life and faith of a family.

The challenge is to encourage, but not force, young people to grow in faith and develop a relationship with God. As children become adolescents, we need to lessen our demands and increase our invitations to religious participation and practice. Sometimes it feels extremely risky to give adolescents a choice, and sometimes it is painful to watch them put God and their spiritual life at the bottom of their list of priorities. When we are discouraged by their choices, we need to remind ourselves that Jesus always invited people to respond, never demanded, and that God will guide us into the future. In these wonderful moments, we can celebrate God's grace.

■ Did you learn anything new in this section about sharing faith with teenagers?

■ How can you use these suggestions to improve the way you share faith with your teenager? What first steps will you take?

A further look

Read the reflection on baptism aloud. Take time to identify symbols or images individually and then share your ideas with the group.

In Baptism, we promise to guide our children in putting on the mind and heart of Christ. As Paul says, "Let the same mind be in you that was in Christ Jesus…"(Philippians 2:5). When we share the stories of Jesus and put their messages into practice in our lives, we are putting on the mind and heart of Christ.

Think of a symbol or image for your family that reflects putting on the mind and heart of Christ. Take time at home to create or find this symbol and display it in a special place to remind everyone of the importance of sharing and living the stories of Jesus.

Wrap-up

See page 9 in the intro-
duction for a description
of "Wrap-up" items. See
page 51 for suggested
closing prayers.

Before you go, take time for the following:

■ **Group ministry task**

■ **Review**

■ **Personal concerns and prayer concerns**

■ **Closing prayers**

Daily walk

Bible readings

Day 1
Exodus 20:1-17

Day 2
Matthew 5:1-11

Day 3
Mark 12:28-34

Day 4
Luke 6:27-38

Day 5
Matthew 25:31-46

Day 6
Romans 12:9-18

Day 7
John 14:6-7, 15-21

Verse for the journey

For I am convinced that neither death, nor life, nor angels, nor
rulers, nor things present, nor things to come, nor powers, nor
height, nor depth, nor anything else in all creation, will be able
to separate us from the love of God in Christ Jesus our Lord.
Romans 8:38-39

Thought for the journey

Values are the important internal compasses that guide us to
make decisions and set priorities. When teenagers have positive values, they grow into caring adults who set high stan-
dards for themselves and the people around them.

Prayer for the journey

O most merciful Redeemer, Friend and Brother;
May I know thee more clearly,
Love thee more dearly,
And follow thee more nearly.
Amen

Richard of Chichester, 1197-1253

3 Celebrating Rituals as a Family

Focus

Have a number of family ritual books available to review during the session. See the resource list on page 54 for suggestions.

Rituals are essential for our family life. Family rituals give us a sense of permanence, the assurance that even the most ordinary of family activities are meaningful and significant.

Community building

Reflect on the questions and share stories with the group.

In this chapter, we will have an opportunity to explore the importance of family rituals and identify rituals to celebrate throughout the year.

Recall one significant religious ritual that your family celebrates alone or with your extended family.

- Why is this ritual meaningful to your family?
- Does your family experience God through this ritual?

Option

Recall one experience of worship or ritual celebration in your church that really moved you. How were you moved? Why was this worship service or ritual celebration meaningful to you? Did you experience God at this time?

Read the psalm together.

Opening prayer

¹ Make a joyful noise to the Lord, all the earth.
² Worship the Lord with gladness;
come into his presence with singing.
³ Know that the Lord is God.
It is he that made us, and we are his;
we are his people, and the sheep of his pasture.
⁴ Enter his gates with thanksgiving,
and his courts with praise.
Give thanks to him, bless his name.
⁵ For the Lord is good;
his steadfast love endures forever,
and his faithfulness to all generations.

Psalm 100

■ Why are rituals so important for healthy family life and for growing in faith as a family?

Ecclesiastes 3:1-2,4,6-7

¹ For everything there is a season, and a time for every matter under heaven:
² a time to be born, and a time to die;
a time to plant, and a time to pluck up what is planted;
⁴ a time to weep, and a time to laugh;
a time to mourn, and a time to dance;
⁶ a time to seek, and a time to lose;
a time to keep, and a time to throw away;
⁷ a time to tear, and a time to sew;
a time to keep silence, and a time to speak;

The importance of ritual

Our family rituals define the unity of our life together. Each family's rituals are a reflection of what the family holds most sacred.

Birthday and anniversary celebrations with special foods or customs, special holiday gatherings, family reunions, and family celebrations around transitional times such as births, marriages, and deaths are all rituals that celebrate important events in our family life. Faith is shared when the presence of God's spirit in these ordinary events is made explicit through shared celebration and ritual. Including simple prayers, music, or Bible readings in our rituals can help to connect the rhythms of our daily lives with God's active presence in our families.

■ What role do rituals play in your life today? In your family's life?

■ What role would you like rituals of faith to play in your family's life?

Daily rituals

Rituals throughout the day help us to recognize and celebrate God's presence in our family life each day. Think about the many opportunities in your daily family life for celebrating a ritual of faith:

    a. Morning or evening prayer
    b. Table blessings (before and after meals)
    c. Reading and discussing Bible stories and how they relate to everyday life

    d. Blessings for leaving times (school, activities, work, a date)

    e. Times of decision-making, thanksgiving, joy, sorrow, failures, and successes

    f. Times of forgiveness and healing

In the constantly changing world of teenagers, daily rituals provide stability and remind us of God's constant presence.

- What daily rituals of faith are observed in your family now?

- Are there any new daily rituals of faith that you would like to introduce in your family?

- How would you introduce a new ritual in your family?

Consider this

The Search Institute has found that adolescents can develop a positive identity when families have a sense of purpose and demonstrate a positive view of the future. Read the descriptions of assets 39 and 40 on page 53.

- **How can these assets connect with your family's rituals?**

Discovery

Seasons of the church year

Read and discuss.

The possibilities for celebrating the seasons of the church year at home are numerous. For example, one family's ritual for Advent involves creating and displaying an Advent wreath. At the beginning of the Advent season, the house is darkened before the evening meal. A family member lights the first candle on the wreath and reads a short scripture passage and prayer. Each week, the family lights an additional candle, and the light around the table grows. In this way, the entire family prepares for the coming of the Messiah at Christmas.

Each season offers opportunities for celebrating rituals at home:

Advent: daily prayers and Scripture readings, Advent wreath

Christmas: Blessing for the Christmas meal, prayer while sharing Christmas gifts

Lent: Ash Wednesday prayer and simple meal, blessing a Lenten home cross, daily prayers and Scripture readings, seder meal, Holy Week Scripture readings

Be sure to consider opportunities for celebrating ethnic holidays and feasts, even those of other ethnic groups.

- How do you currently celebrate the seasons of the church year in your family?

- What are some new possibilities for celebrating the seasons of the church year in your family?

- How would you introduce new church year celebrations into your family life?

Life transitions and milestones

Simple prayerful celebrations of life transitions and milestones help teenagers recognize God's presence in their lives. Think about the possibilities in your family for celebrating birthdays, baptism anniversaries, wedding anniversaries, Mother's Day, Father's Day, beginning high school, starting a new job, getting a driver's license, graduating from high school, and leaving for college, the military, or work.

- How do you currently celebrate transitions and milestones in your family?

- What are some new possibilities for celebrating life transitions and milestones in your family?

- How would you introduce rituals for life transitions and milestones into your family life?

Suggestions for celebrating rituals with teenagers

Read and discuss.

The experiences of teenagers provide many opportunities to create and celebrate new ritual expressions and rites of passage as a family. Here are several suggestions to help you celebrate family rituals with teenagers.

a. Involve all family members in planning and celebrating the event.
b. If celebrating ritual moments is new to your family, start small. Choose an event or occasion that marks a real turning point in your life as a family (a first job or getting a learner's permit, for example) and mark it with a simple but festive meal that includes

a prayer or reading, reflection or storytelling, and a short blessing. If your family has made a habit of sharing rituals, know that some of your "traditional" family rituals will fall to the wayside during adolescence as your family grows and changes.

c. While the ritual may focus on an event of particular significance for one family member, the way you celebrate should be meaningful for everyone and remind them of the family's interconnectedness.

d. Celebrate special moments for your older adolescent in ways that relate to adolescents. Incorporate music, food, readings, and stories that speak to your son or daughter.

e. Involve family friends in your ritual sharing. Invite key members of your extended family and your adolescent's special friends to take part. Hospitality is a treasured trait in healthy families.

f. Keep the sharing and ritual simple and straightforward. Celebrate events that are central to your life as a family.

g. Do not force participation. Schedule the celebration for a time that is convenient for all family members. If one family member chooses not to take part, go ahead anyway.

A further look

Set up a prayer table with a large white candle, Bible, bowl of water, and a small bowl of olive oil. Light the candle as you begin. Play instrumental music in the background.

Recalling the baptismal celebration

In this chapter we will remember baptism through a prayer service.

Gather prayerfully around the prayer table.

Read the baptism of Jesus in Mark 1:9-11.

As one person holds the bowl of water, one by one each person dips his or her hand in the water and makes of the sign of the cross. Conclude by praying, "May these waters renew the grace of our baptism in each one of us."

Pass the small bowl of olive oil around the group. One by one, dip your hand in the oil and make the sign of the cross on your forehead. As each does this, everyone prays: "May Christ strengthen you with his love and power."

Close by reading Psalm 23.

Wrap-up

Before you go, take time for the following:

- Group ministry task

- Review

- Personal concerns and prayer concerns

- Closing prayers

Daily walk

Bible readings

Day 1
Luke 22:7-20

Day 2
Acts 2:37-42

Day 3
Psalm 95:1-7

Day 4
Acts 2:43-47

Day 5
Psalm 63:1-8

Day 6
Mark 1:9-11

Day 7
Micah 6:6-8

Verse for the journey

O come, let us worship and bow down,
let us kneel before the Lord, our Maker!
Psalm 95:6

Thought for the journey

In the constantly changing world of teenagers, daily rituals provide stability and remind us of God's constant presence.

Prayer for the journey

Lord, guide us as we celebrate the seasons of faith in our family. Draw us closer together as we celebrate your presence throughout our day and throughout our year.
Amen

4 Praying as a Family

Focus

Have a number of prayer resources for families with older adolescents available to review. See the list on page 54 for suggestions.

Prayer is the very heart of our encounter and relationship with God. If prayer constitutes the soul of the Christian spiritual life, prayer must lie at the center of family spirituality.

Community building

Reflect and discuss.

Option

Describe your prayer life today using a color, a song or hymn, a weather condition, or a part of nature (sunset, mountains, ocean).

This chapter explores the role of prayer in your life and the life of your family. It offers a variety of suggestions for strengthening the prayer life of families with teenagers. We begin by reflecting on the role of prayer in the life of your family today.

- Does your family pray? When? If your family prays regularly, what do you pray for or about?

- Can you think of a time when your family felt close to God?

Read the psalm together.

Opening prayer

¹ It is good to give thanks to the Lord,
to sing praises to your name, O Most High;
² to declare your steadfast love in the morning,
and your faithfulness by night,
³ to the music of the lute and the harp,
to the melody of the lyre.
⁴ For you, O Lord, have made me glad by your work;
at the works of your hands I sing for joy.

Psalm 92:1-4

Romans 8:26-27

26 the Spirit helps us in our weakness; for we do not know how to pray as we ought, but that very Spirit intercedes with sighs too deep for words. 27 And God, who searches the heart, knows what is the mind of the Spirit, because the Spirit intercedes for the saints according to the will of God.

What is prayer?

■ How do you define prayer? Write a definition of prayer that reflects how you understand and pray at the present time.

■ What circumstances or events cause you to pray? When do you feel closest to God: alone, in a church setting, in a group, or in nature?

Read and discuss.

In his book, *Prayer—Beginning Conversations with God* (Minneapolis: Augsburg, 1995, pages 7-8), Richard Beckmen writes a definition for prayer:

"Some people think prayer is 'saying a prayer'—speaking a particular intention to God. Prayer, however, can be understood more generally than that. Prayer, in a broad sense, links all aspects of our lives to God. God is present in all of life. We might set aside certain times and places for worship, but God is not absent from any time or any place. It is right and proper to pray at all times and in all places.

"Prayer is the name we give to the experience of being in communication with God wherever we are and whatever we are doing. Prayer is experience because it involves our senses, minds, souls, and spirits. When we pray, we know that this is happening. Prayer is a point of interaction with God."

■ Did you discover anything new in this definition of prayer?

■ What is your biggest obstacle to prayer? What would you like to do to strengthen your own prayer life?

■ From your perspective, what is your son or daughter's biggest obstacle to prayer?

Discovery

Encouraging teenagers to pray

- Why should prayer be an important part of your teenager's life?

- Why should prayer be an important part of your family's life?

- If prayer is part of your family life, how and when do you pray with your teen? How do you encourage your son or daughter to pray?

Read and discuss.

In *Face to Face with God in Your Home: Guiding Children and Youth in Prayer* (Minneapolis: Augsburg Fortress, 1995), Carolyn Luetjue and Meg Marcrander discuss how to encourage teenagers to pray:

"Teenagers understand prayer as conversation with God. They can begin to think more deeply about their own prayer experiences as they relate to God as friend and confidant. They will benefit from seeing their parents and other adult role models praying comfortably and using prayer in all areas of their life. When teenagers observe their parents speaking to God regularly they will be more likely to make prayer an integral part of their own spiritual growth" (p. 97).

"Teach your teenagers that there are many ways to pray. We can pray formally, kneeling with eyes closed and hands folded. We can also pray while jogging or studying for a test. Our prayers can include words of sorrow and pain, expressions of joy and thankfulness, or confessions of guilt and unworthiness. Help your adolescent understand that prayer is simply a conversation with a loving, forgiving, and understanding friend. Our friend Jesus promises to be there always to listen to and answer our prayers" (p. 81).

How can we help teenagers become praying people? Here are several suggestions:

Jesus and prayer: Explore the Gospels to help young people discover when and how Jesus prays and what he teaches us about prayer.

Read about Jesus' teachings on prayer: Luke 11:1-13 and Matthew 6:5-15, 7:7-11; Luke 10:21-22; Matthew 11:25-30.

Read about times when Jesus prayed: Mark 1:32-39, Luke 5:15-16, Luke 6:12-13, Luke 9:18-20, Luke 22:39-46 or Matthew 26:36-46 or Mark 14:32-42; Matthew 14:22-23 or Mark 6:45-46, John 17.

A variety of prayer experiences: Encourage your son or daughter to experience and use a variety of prayer forms:

Prayers of praise in which we give praise to God for being good, for the mystery and majesty of God.

Prayers of thanksgiving in which we give thanks for all our blessings in life.

Spontaneous prayers in which we offer God what is in our hearts and minds.

Prayers of petition in which we ask God for what we as well as others need.

Prayers of contrition in which we ask God for forgiveness and healing for our wrongdoing.

Praying about issues and problems: One of the gifts of prayer is that we can confide all our problems and concerns in God, who promises to hear and respond. Pray with your teenager, aloud and in silence, about the issues and conflicts he or she faces.

Praying with Scripture: In your prayers, use Scripture passages that address the concerns and experiences of young people. Here are several suggestions from Psalms:

Psalm 8:1-7 *(our place in God's creation)*
Psalm 11:1-7 and 62:1-12 *(trust in God)*
Psalm 16:1-11 and 139:1-12 *(Lord's presence)*
Psalm 25:1-14 and 32:1-11 *(forgiveness)*
Psalm 30:1-12 *(thanksgiving)*
Psalm 63:1-8 *(longing for God)*
Psalm 103:1-14 *(praise of God)*
Psalm 121:1-8 *(help)*

Praying about decisions: A helpful tool for solving emotionally-charged issues is to pray about the situations ahead of time. This provides the reflection time needed to make good decisions. It also allows the young person to place the decision before God and seek guidance.

Personal prayer time: Encourage your teen to develop a personal prayer time each day when he or she can speak and listen to God silently and privately. A prayer journal can be created for favorite prayers, Scripture passages, photos, artwork, prayer lists and requests, and personal thoughts.

Family prayer time: In the midst of your busy lives, commit to finding a few moments to quietly spend with one another in prayer.

Prayer concerns list: Keep a family prayer list where everyone in the family will see it. Encourage family members to write brief notes about problems or situations for which they would like the family to pray, as well as the names of people for whom they would like the family to pray.

Above all, we can encourage our sons and daughters to pray by being praying people ourselves. We may find that our older adolescents can teach us about prayer and encourage us to be praying people as well.

- In the list above, did you learn anything new about encouraging teenagers to pray? Is there anything you would add to this list?

- Which suggestions would you like to focus on with your teenager?

- Have you learned anything about prayer from your son or daughter?

Reflecting on faith in daily life

If time allows, practice the "Reflecting on Faith in Daily Life" prayer form as a group.

In order for us to teach teenagers and ourselves to look at the world through the eyes of faith, we can practice faith reflection in our daily lives. Faith reflection helps us discover God's presence in our experience, the difference God's presence makes, and what God expects. It is a simple but effective way to teach young people to develop their inner spiritual lives.

Practice this process together with your teenager. Encourage your son or daughter to also use the process as part of his or her personal prayer time.

Selecting an experience. Each day of family life is filled with hundreds of human interactions and the potential for acts of love, service, compassion, and forgiveness. How can we discover God's presence in our daily lives? Look for the "important" events. "Firsts" and "lasts" in family life are often significant because they involve transitions (and sometimes crises) that can serve to connect us or drive us apart from each other and the Lord. New learning is always significant as are important encounters with a special person or place.

Describing the experience. In describing the experience, we need to know who was involved. What happened? Where did the event take place? When? How?

Entering the experience. To enter the experience, close your eyes and try to relive it in your mind. First, identify your feelings, thoughts, and actions at the time of the experience and then visualize the experience in your mind as if it were being played on a movie screen. Identify your present feelings and thoughts as you do this.

Learning from the experience. After reliving the experience, ask yourself how you see God present in the experience. Try to relate the experience to a particular Scripture passage, Christian belief, tradition or church teaching. Does the experience illustrate God's love for you? Is it an example of being one in Christ's body or an example of Christ's resurrection in today's world? Why is it important to you? What have you learned?

A further look

Baptism immerses us into a life with God who is Three in One: God our parent and provider, Jesus our redeemer and friend, and the Holy Spirit our sanctifier and consolation. The Lord's Prayer connects us to this life, reminding us of who we are and what our Christian lives are all about.

Pray the Lord's Prayer (a version familiar to you) and then a contemporary adaptation of Lord's Prayer such as this one:

"O Most Compassionate Life-giver, may we honor and praise you; may we work with you to establish your new order of justice, peace and love.

Give us what we need for growth and help us, through forgiving others, to accept forgiveness.

Strengthen us in the time of testing, that we may resist all evil, for all the tenderness, strength, and love are yours, now and forever. Amen."

(Adaptation of the Lord's Prayer by Bill Wallace.
From: *Gifts of Many Cultures.* Maren Tirabassi and Kathy Wonson Eddy.
Cleveland: United Church Press, 1995. page 49)

Wrap-up

Before you go, take time for the following:

- Group ministry task

- Review

- Personal concerns and prayer concerns

- Closing prayers

Daily walk

Bible readings

Day 1
Psalm 148

Day 2
Psalm 116

Day 3
Psalm 42

Day 4
Psalm 71

Day 5
Psalm 20

Day 6
Psalm 111

Day 7
Psalm 143

Verse for the journey

Ask, and it will be given you; search, and you will find; knock, and the door will be opened for you. For everyone who asks receives, and everyone who searches finds, and for everyone who knocks, the door will be opened. Matthew 7:7-8

Thought for the journey

Prayer is the name we give to the experience of being in communication with God wherever we are and whatever we are doing.

Richard Beckmen, *Prayer—Beginning Conversations with God*,
Minneapolis: Augsburg, 1995, page 8

Prayer for the journey

Lord,
Make me an instrument of your peace.
Where there is hatred, let me sow love;
Where there is injury, pardon;
Where there is doubt, faith;
Where there is despair, hope;
Where there is darkness, light;
Where there is sadness, joy.

Francis of Assisi, 1182-1226

5 Serving as a Family

Focus

Have a number of service books available to review. See the resource list on page 54 for suggestions. It would also be helpful to have a list of church and community service projects for older adolescents and their families.

The calls to serve and work for justice are central themes in the Bible. When families serve the needs of others, they follow in the footsteps of Jesus and grow in faith as a family.

Community building

Option

Complete the following unfinished sentences.

■ **For me, service means...**

■ **A social problem I wish we could fix is...**

■ **The world would be a better place if...**

■ **A person who embodies a life of justice and service is...**

■ **It is important for Christians to serve others because...**

■ **In the past, I was involved in serving others when...**

Reflect on what society says about the following items. Use a phrase from a popular commercial or advertisement if possible. Then comment on what Jesus says about these items.

- a. money
- b. success
- c. physical appearance
- d. power
- e. immediate gratification
- f. possessions
- g. equality
- h. peace and forgiveness
- i. pain and sorrow
- j. poverty

Opening prayer

Lord, teach us what it means to be "poor in spirit" in a consumer society; to comfort those who suffer in our midst; to "show mercy" in an often unforgiving world; to "hunger and thirst for justice" in a nation still challenged by hunger and homelessness, poverty and prejudice; and to be "peacemakers" in an often violent and fearful world. Amen

The following Scripture passage contains the Beatitudes, statements from Jesus' Sermon on the Mount.

Form two groups. Have one group read the odd-numbered verses aloud. The second group reads the even-numbered verses.

Matthew 5:3-12

3 **"Blessed are the poor in spirit, for theirs is the kingdom of heaven.**
4 **"Blessed are those who mourn, for they will be comforted.**
5 **"Blessed are the meek, for they will inherit the earth.**
6 **"Blessed are those who hunger and thirst for righteousness, for they will be filled.**
7 **"Blessed are the merciful, for they will receive mercy.**
8 **"Blessed are the pure in heart, for they will see God.**
9 **"Blessed are the peacemakers, for they will be called children of God.**
10 **"Blessed are those who are persecuted for righteousness' sake, for theirs is the kingdom of heaven.**
11 **"Blessed are you when people revile you and persecute you and utter all kinds of evil against you falsely on my account. 12 Rejoice and be glad, for your reward is great in heaven, for in the same way they persecuted the prophets who were before you."**

Read and discuss.

Living the Beatitudes

In our day, just as in Jesus' day, the values contained in the Beatitudes run counter to the prevailing values of society.

- How does Jesus' wisdom compare with what our society says?

- How does your family embody the Beatitudes in daily life? Which of the Beatitudes are strengths in your family? Where do you need to grow as a family? How will you do this?

- How can you assist your teenager in living the Beatitudes in daily life?

Review assets 9, 26, and 27, and the benefits of service. Then discuss the questions.

Consider this

Three of the 40 assets for healthy development explicitly focus on the importance of the service: #9 service to others, #26 family values caring, and #27 family values equality and social justice. Read about these on pages 52-53.

The research and work of the Search Institute shows that serving others has the following benefits:

Helps make the Christian faith real.

Promotes healthy lifestyles and choices.

Assists in the development of positive self-esteem, self-confidence, and social skills.

Helps people discover their personal gifts and abilities.

Teaches new skills and perspectives.

Nurtures a lifelong commitment to service and justice.

Builds a stronger sense of community within the family and among families who serve.

Impacts the people who are served.

Improves the quality of life and the climate of the community.

- What do you see as the most important benefits of serving for your older adolescent?

- What do you see as the most important benefits of serving for your family?

Living out justice and service

Take time for everyone to read this section silently. Then discuss the questions.

Justice for all God's people and service to those in need, especially the poor, was central to Jesus' life, teaching, and ministry and is at the heart of discipleship and life as a Christian today. As parents of teenagers, this dimension of faith can be incorporated into our parenting and family life in a variety of ways.

Actions of direct service are a good starting point for families with older adolescents because they involve young people in addressing specific needs—food, shelter, clothing, health care, and education. Being involved with service projects allows older adolescents to give of themselves and see the results of their efforts. As parents, we can help our sons and daughters to discover that they are important and that God can use their gifts, talents, and energy right now.

It is important to assist teenagers in understanding the need to change those situations that make people victims of injustice in the first place. For example, families with adolescents who are working at a homeless shelter or soup kitchen could also be involved with a local coalition that is working to create housing, employment, and just policies for the homeless.

Families with older adolescents can put their faith into practice by:

a. promoting positive ways to resolve conflict within the family and the community.
b. learning about and discussing important social issues and the Bible's teachings on justice, peace, and service.
c. caring for the earth and its resources.
d. sharing family time, talents, and possessions with people in need.
e. standing in opposition to violence.
f. living simply and taking good care of personal and family possessions.
g. praying regularly for greater justice and peace, and for those in need.
h. participating in service projects as a family.
i. involving teenagers in a variety of service projects, including summer weeklong service programs.
j. making financial donations to support the efforts of local and national groups working for justice for the poor.

k. supporting public policies that protect life, promote dignity, preserve creation, and build peace.
l. working with other families to work for greater charity, justice, and peace.

Another important role of parents is to encourage and support the service involvements of their older adolescents, from driving them to service projects to helping them raise money for a summer service trip.

- How are older adolescents and families with older adolescents already involved in service in your church and community?

- How is your congregation engaged in the work of justice and service?

- What organizations in your community are engaged in the work of justice and service? Who do they serve?

- How can your older adolescent and your family become involved in justice and service—locally and globally?

A further look

Have someone read this section aloud. Then take time to think about the pledge and share ideas. During the week, discuss the pledge and complete it with all members of your family.

A family commitment to serve

Baptism empowers us for our mission as Christians. Each of us has unique abilities, a certain amount of time, and financial resources. Are there changes that you can make in allocating your talent, time, and treasure so that you can more effectively serve those in need and promote the work of justice—locally, nationally, globally?

Reaffirm your baptismal mission with a family pledge for justice and service.

A Pledge

This is what God asks of you, and only this:
That you act justly, love tenderly,
and walk humbly with your God. Micah 6:8

In our attempt to act justly and serve those in need, our family will...

Wrap-up

Before you go, take time for the following:

- Group ministry task

- Review

- Personal concerns and prayer concerns

- Closing prayers

Daily walk

Bible readings

Day 1
Isaiah 2:1-4

Day 2
Psalm 146

Day 3
Luke 4:16-21

Day 4
Luke 10:25-37

Day 5
Acts 4:32-35

Day 6
John 13:1-15

Day 7
1 John 4:19-21

Verse for the journey

For I was hungry and you gave me food, I was thirsty and you gave me something to drink, I was a stranger and you welcomed me, I was naked and you gave me clothing, I was sick and you took care of me, I was in prison and you visited me. Just as you did it to one of the least of these who are members of my family, you did it to me. Matthew 25:35-36, 40

Thought for the journey

As parents, we can help our sons and daughters to discover that they are important and that God can use their gifts, talents, and energy right now.

Prayer for the journey

God, true light and source of all light, may we recognize you in oppressed people and poor people, in homeless people and hungry people. May we be open to your Spirit so that we can be a means of healing, strength, and peace for all your people. Inspire us to use the varied gifts with which we have been blessed in the service of others. We ask this in the name of Jesus, your son.
Amen

6 Relating as a Family

Have a number of parenting and family enrichment resources available. See the list on page 54 for suggestions.

Focus

Solid parenting skills and effective communication are two essential ingredients for nurturing the growth of older adolescents and building a strong family life.

Community building

Reflect on the statements individually, then share responses with the group.

- One of my greatest gifts or strengths as a parent of an older adolescent is…

- Tell a story that illustrates one of your parenting gifts or strengths.

- One thing I would like to learn in order to be a better parent of an older adolescent…

Option

Describe your family life today using a TV commercial, TV show, Broadway musical or feature film, popular song, or popular book title.

Opening prayer

Gracious God, give us the strength and wisdom to build families on the foundations of love and compassion, kindness and generosity, humility and gentleness, forgiveness and peace. Amen

Have someone read the
Scripture passage aloud.

■ What are the qualities you want to demonstrate to your older adolescent by the way you live?

Colossians 3:12-15

12 As God's chosen ones, holy and beloved, clothe yourselves with compassion, kindness, humility, meekness, and patience. 13 Bear with one another and, if anyone has a complaint against another, forgive each other; just as the Lord has forgiven you, so you also must forgive. 14 Above all, clothe yourselves with love, which binds everything together in perfect harmony. 15 And let the peace of Christ rule in your hearts, to which indeed you were called in the one body. And be thankful.

■ Is there a quality you would like to develop in yourself as a parent?

Parenting teenagers

As a group, develop a
list of the characteristics
of effective parenting.

■ The characteristics of effective parenting of older adolescents are…

One of the most effective ways to create a strong family is through the example of our life as parents—our faith, values, attitudes, and skills. It is so important to remember that parenting skills are learned. Through the support and encouragement of other parents, by developing an understanding of your older adolescent, through reading and taking courses, and through our own practice of parenting, we learn how to be effective parents of older adolescents.

Read the following characteristics of effective parenting of older adolescents. Are any of these items on your list of characteristics? Is there anything you would add?

Show your love. Unconditional love should be the basis for every parenting decision and action.

Recognize that affection is continuous communication. It is love without words. Teach through your example; practice what you preach. Model the faith and values you want your older adolescent to adopt.

Look through an older adolescent's eyes. Learn to share the reasons behind the decisions and choices you make and seek to find out why they do what they do.

Invest the time. Making family a priority fosters an older adolescent's self-esteem and sense of belonging.

Listen before you talk. Talk less and listen more. Become aware of your older adolescent's prime times to talk and arrange to be present at those times.

Don't try to be a perfect parent. Good parents become better through mistakes.

Parent in the present. Second-guessing yourself or dwelling on the uncertain future will erode your confidence and ability to give your best to your older adolescent today.

Laugh whenever and wherever you can. Humor helps maintain perspective and eases anxiety.

Allow your older adolescent to have a voice in family decisions whenever possible. Being consulted makes an older adolescent feel like an integral part of the family.

Encourage your older adolescent to live up to his or her capabilities.

■ What new practices would you like to begin in your parenting? How will you do this?

Read and discuss.

Consider this

Many of the 40 assets from Search Institute describe skills that are necessary for effective family life and for the healthy growth of older adolescents. Explore the following assets: 1, 2, 11, 32, 33, 35, 36, 37, 38, 39 and 40. (See pages 52-53 for the list of assets.)

■ **How important are these assets for nurturing the positive growth of older adolescents?**

■ **How can you strengthen these assets in your family? What can you do to promote these assets and skills in the life of your older adolescent?**

Communicating effectively with older adolescents

- The hardest thing about communicating with my older adolescent is…

- Two of the topics or issues that are the most difficult to discuss with my older adolescent are…

- The best way to communicate with my older adolescent is…

Select a topic or issue that parents and older adolescents have difficulty discussing. Do a role-play on this topic, with one member of the group playing a parent and another playing an older adolescent. To use the role-play effectively, follow these guidelines:

1. Clearly define the situation and have players assume their roles.
2. Stop the action before the role-play is exhausted.
3. Discuss and evaluate the role-play: name central turning points and outcomes; ask for insights and feedback from the role-players; and identify important issues and insights.

Even when parents and older adolescents consciously make time for one another, they sometimes find it difficult to connect with each other's thoughts and feelings. New experiences and relationships demand new ways of communicating. Learning new approaches to communication can be an important step in helping the relationship with your older adolescent to grow and flourish. Here are several suggestions for improving your communication skills.

First, take time to establish relationships. Time together can mean going to a special event or sharing an activity you both enjoy as a way to get to know each other better.

Second, recognize and reduce roadblocks to effective communication. Without realizing it, we as parents sometimes set up roadblocks to communication with our older adolescents. Some of the most common obstacles to communication for parents and older adolescents are:

Share responses to the statements, then develop a list of key ingredients for effective communication with older adolescents.

If you choose, the role-play activity can be repeated using different topics and players.

Read and discuss.

a. *Lack of time.* Communication is often handled "on the run" without taking the time needed to help everyone involved understand the situation, the relationships, and the issues at stake.

b. *Changes normal to adolescence.* Older adolescents can go through times of growing self-consciousness, limited verbal skills, increased independence, and growing resistance to authority.

c. *Inappropriate and ineffective methods of communicating.* Belittling the importance of the issue, criticizing or ridiculing, judging or blaming, giving too many orders or too much advice, offering solutions before the issues have been talked through adequately together, threatening, and preaching all hinder good communication.

Third, seek first to understand, and then to be understood. Listen for the feelings and meaning in what your older adolescent says. Communication is truly effective when there is a balance between your desire to understand others and to be understood by them.

Fourth, understand and accept where older adolescents are at developmentally. It is natural for older adolescents to appear more self-centered at times or to push the limits in order to become more autonomous. Simply asking a "feeling" question, such as "How do you feel about..." may open new dimensions in conversations.

Finally, focus on the concerns and interests of the teens. A general question or comment on any of the following topics could generate a good conversation:

Family matters: decisions and issues that affect older adolescents and the whole family

Controversial issues: sexuality, drugs and alcohol, and so forth

Fears: the future, being a success, being accepted, using new freedoms, accepting responsibility for their lives

The future: jobs, careers, technical school or college

Current events: news, issues, and problems in the community, nation, and world

Personal interests and concerns: activities such as sports, hobbies, friends, school; concerns about their looks, school performance, or losing a parent or best friend

- Did you learn anything new in this section about communicating with teenagers?
- How can you improve your communication skills?
- What first steps will you take?

Personal parenting creed

To apply the insights on family life and effective parenting from this chapter, develop "A Parent of an Older Adolescent Creed." During the weeks following this small group meeting, discuss these sentences with your older adolescent and ask for his or her ideas:

- As a parent of an older adolescent, I believe…
- As a parent of an older adolescent, I will…

A further look

Have someone read this section aloud.

Baptism connection

In baptism, we are given a new birth by water and the Holy Spirit. In his letter to the Galatians, Paul challenges us to live in the Spirit. As Paul writes in Galatians, "the fruit of the Spirit is love, joy, peace, patience, kindness, generosity, faithfulness, gentleness, and self-control" (Galatians 5:22-23).

- Do you see any of these fruits or qualities in your family now?

Take a moment for prayer. Reflect on which of these fruits your family most needs now. Pray to the Holy Spirit to respond to your need.

Wrap-up

Before you go, take time for the following:

- Group ministry task

- Review

- Personal concerns and prayer concerns

- Closing prayers

Daily walk

Bible readings

Day 1
Romans 12:9-13

Day 2
John 15:12-17

Day 3
1 Corinthians 13:1-13

Day 4
Luke 6:37-38

Day 5
Philippians 2:1-11

Day 6
Ephesians 4:1-6

Day 7
Deuteronomy 6:1-9

Verse for the journey

Love is patient; love is kind; love is not envious or boastful or arrogant or rude. It does not insist on its own way; it is not irritable or resentful; it does not rejoice in wrongdoing, but rejoices in the truth. It bears all things, believes all things, hopes all things, endures all things. 1 Corinthians 13:4-7

Thought for the journey

One of the keys to a strong family is communication that is clear, open, frequent, and honest.

Prayer for the journey

Lord, give our family the strength and courage to listen and communicate clearly, to forgive and comfort compassionately, and to love each other abundantly.
Amen

Appendix

Group directory

Record information about group members here.

Name	Address	Phone number

Prayers

■ Closing Prayer

Lord God, you have called your servants to ventures of which we cannot see the ending, by paths as yet untrodden, through perils unknown. Give us faith to go out with good courage, not knowing where we go, but only that your hand is leading us and your love supporting us; through Jesus Christ our Lord. Amen

From *Lutheran Book of Worship* (page 153) copyright © 1978.

(If you plan to pray the Lord's Prayer, record the version your group uses in the next column.)

■ The Lord's Prayer

Group commitments

Do not be conformed to this world, but be transformed by the renewing of your minds, so that you may discern what is the will of God—what is good and acceptable and perfect. Romans 12:2.

- For our time together, we have made the following commitments to each other

- Goals for our study of this topic are

- Our group ministry task is

- My personal action plan is

Prayer requests

_____

_____

_____

_____

_____

_____

_____

_____

_____

_____

_____

40 Developmental Assets for Adolescents

EXTERNAL ASSETS

ASSET TYPE	ASSET NAME	ASSET DEFINITION
Support	1. Family support	Family life provides high levels of love and support.
	2. Positive family communication	Young person and her or his parent(s) communicate positively, and young person is willing to seek advice and counsel from parent(s).
	3. Other adult relationships	Young person receives support from three or more nonparent adults.
	4. Caring neighborhood	Young person experiences caring neighbors.
	5. Caring school climate	School provides a caring, encouraging environment.
	6. Parent involvement in schooling	Parent(s) are actively involved in helping young person succeed in school.
Empowerment	7. Community values youth	Young person perceives that adults in the community value youth.
	8. Youth as resources	Young people are given useful roles in the community.
	9. Service to others	Young person serves in the community one hour or more per week.
	10. Safety	Young person feels safe at home, at school, and in the neighborhood.
Boundaries and Expectations	11. Family boundaries	Family has clear rules and consequences, and monitors the young person's whereabouts.
	12. School boundaries	School provides clear rules and consequences.
	13. Neighborhood boundaries	Neighbors take responsibility for monitoring young people's behavior.
	14. Adult role models	Parent(s) and other adults model positive, responsible behavior.
	15. Positive peer influence	Young person's best friends model responsible behavior.
	16. High expectations	Both parent(s) and teachers encourage the young person to do well.
Constructive Use of Time	17. Creative activities	Young person spends three or more hours per week in lessons or practice in music, theater, or other arts.
	18. Youth programs	Young person spends three or more hours per week in sports, clubs, or organizations at school and/or in community organizations.
	19. Religious community	Young person spends one hour or more per week in activities in a religious institution.
	20. Time at home	Young person is out with friends "with nothing special to do" two or fewer nights per week.

INTERNAL ASSETS

ASSET TYPE	ASSET NAME	ASSET DEFINITION
Commitment to Learning	21. Achievement motivation	Young person is motivated to do well in school.
	22. School engagement	Young person is actively engaged in learning.
	23. Homework	Young person reports doing at least one hour of homework every school day.
	24. Bonding to school	Young person cares about her or his school.
	25. Reading for pleasure	Young person reads for pleasure three or more hours per week.
Positive Values	26. Caring	Young person places high value on helping other people.
	27. Equality and social justice	Young person places high value on promoting equality and reducing hunger and poverty.
	28. Integrity	Young person acts on convictions and stands up for her or his beliefs.
	29. Honesty	Young person "tells the truth even when it is not easy."
	30. Responsibility	Young person accepts and takes personal responsibility.
	31. Restraint	Young person believes it is important not to be sexually active or to use alcohol or other drugs.
Social Competencies	32. Planning and decision making	Young person knows how to plan ahead and make choices.
	33. Interpersonal competence	Young person has empathy, sensitivity, and friendship skills.
	34. Cultural competence	Young person has knowledge of and comfort with people of different cultural/racial/ethnic backgrounds.
	35. Resistance skills	Young person can resist negative peer pressure and dangerous situations.
	36. Peaceful conflict resolution	Young person seeks to resolve conflict nonviolently.
Positive Identity	37. Personal power	Young person feels he or she has control over "things that happen to me."
	38. Self-esteem	Young person reports having a high self-esteem.
	39. Sense of purpose	Young person reports that "my life has a purpose."
	40. Positive view of personal future	Young person is optimistic about her or his personal future.

Benson, Peter, Judy Galbraith and Pamela Espeland. *What Kids Need to Succeed.* Minneapolis: Free Spirit Publishing, 1998.

_____. *What Teens Need to Succeed.* Minneapolis: Free Spirit Publishing, 1998.

Burke, Ray and Ron Herron. *Common Sense Parenting.* Boys Town, NE: Boys Town Press, 1996.

Chesto, Kathleen. *Family Prayer for Family Times—Traditions, Celebrations, and Rituals.* Mystic, CT: Twenty-third Publications, 1996.

Covey, Stephen. *The Seven Habits of Highly Effective Families.* New York: Golden Books, 1997.

Finley, Mitch and Kathy. *Building Christian Families.* Allen, TX: Thomas More/Tabor, 1996.

Fuchs-Kreimer, Rabbi Nancy. *Parenting as Spiritual Journey—Deepening Ordinary and Extraordinary Events into Sacred Occasions.* Woodstock, VT: Jewish Lights Publishing, 1996.

Glenn, H. Stephen, and Jane Nelson. *Raising Self-Reliant Children in a Self-Indulgent World: Seven Building Blocks for Developing Capable Young People.* Rocklin, CA: Prima Publishing & Communications, 2000.

Kallestad, Walter. *The Everyday Anytime Guide to Prayer.* Minneapolis: Augsburg, 1995.

McCarty, Robert. *Tips for Raising Teens—A Primer for Parents.* New York: Paulist Press, 1998.

McGinnis, James and Kathleen. *Parenting for Peace and Justice.* Maryknoll, NY: Orbis Books, 1981.

McGinnis, James, Ken and Gretchen Lovingood, and Jim Vogt. *Families Creating a Circle of Peace.* St.Louis: Families Against Violence Advocacy Network/Institute for Peace and Justice, 1996.

Nelson, Gertrud Mueller. *To Dance with God—Family Ritual and Community Celebration.* New York: Paulist Press, 1986.

Paulson, Terry, and Sean D. Paulson. *Can I Have the Keys to the Car? How Teens and Parents Can Talk about Things that Really Matter.* Minneapolis: Augsburg, 1999.

Payden, Deborah Alberswerth and Laura Loving. *Celebrating at Home—Prayers and Liturgies for Families.* Cleveland: United Church Press, 1998.

Saso, Patt and Steve. *10 Best Gifts for Your Teen.* Notre Dame, IN: Ave Maria Press, 1999.

Seo, Danny. *Heaven on Earth—15 Minute Miracles to Change the World.* New York: Pocket Books, 1999.

Sorensen, David A., and Barbara DeGrote-Sorensen. *Escaping the Family Time Trap: A Practical Guide for Over-Busy Families.* Minneapolis: Augsburg, 2001.

Stinnett, Nick, and Michael O'Donnell. *Good Kids—How You and Your Kids Can Successfully Navigate the Teen Years.* New York: Doubleday, 1996.

Thompson, Marjorie. *Family—The Forming Center.* Nashville: Upper Room Books, 1996.

Wiederkehr, Macrina, OSB. *Seasons of Your Heart.* Morristown, NJ: Silver Burdett Co, 1979.

Wright, Wendy. *Sacred Dwelling—A Spirituality of Family Life.* New York: Crossroad, 1990.

Young, Peter. *Celebrate Life—Rituals for Home and Church.* Cleveland: United Church Press, 1999.

See the Center for Ministry Development's website at cmdnet.org for more resources for parents and children.

See the Search Institute's website at www.search-institute.org for more information on the 40 developmental assets for growth.

Please tell us about your experience with INTERSECTIONS.

4. What I like best about my INTERSECTIONS experience is

5. Three things I want to see the same in future INTERSECTIONS books are

6. Three things I might change in future INTERSECTIONS books are

7. Topics I would like developed for new INTERSECTIONS books are

8. Our group had ____ sessions for the six chapters of this book.

9. Other comments I have about INTERSECTIONS are

Thank you for taking the time to fill out and return this questionnaire.

------------------------- FOLD CARD IN HERE, SEAL WITH TAPE, AND MAIL TODAY! -------------------------

Name _____

Address _____

Daytime telephone _____

Please check the INTERSECTIONS book you are evaluating.

☐ **The Bible and Life**
☐ **Caring and Community**
☐ **Death and Grief**
☐ **Faith**
☐ **Following Jesus**
☐ **Integrity**
☐ **Jesus: Divine and Human**
☐ **Managing Stress**

☐ **Parenting**
☐ **Parenting: Raising Faithful Preschoolers**
☐ **Parenting: Raising Faithful Grade-schoolers**
☐ **Parenting: Raising Faithful Younger Adolescents**

☐ **Parenting: Raising Faithful Older Adolescents**
☐ **Peace**
☐ **Praying**
☐ **Reconcilable Differences**
☐ **Smart Choices**

Please tell us about your small group.

1. Our group had an average attendance of _____.

2. Our group was made up of
____ Young adults (19-25 years).
____ Adults (most between 25-45 years).
____ Adults (most between 45-60 years).
____ Adults (most between 60-75 years).
____ Adults (most 75 and over).
____ Adults (wide mix of ages).
____ Men (number) and ____ women (number).

3. Our group (answer as many as apply)
____ came together for the sole purpose of studying this INTERSECTIONS book.
____ has decided to study another INTERSECTIONS book.
____ is an ongoing Sunday school group.
____ met at a time other than Sunday morning.
____ had only one facilitator for this study.

BUSINESS REPLY MAIL

FIRST-CLASS MAIL   PERMIT NO. 22120   MINNEAPOLIS, MN

POSTAGE WILL BE PAID BY ADDRESSEE

Augsburg Fortress

ATTN INTERSECTIONS TEAM
PO BOX 1209
MINNEAPOLIS MN 55440-8807